BE STILL

JUDY TAYLOR

To my husband, the love of my life and my best friend.

INTRODUCTION

I was raised in darkness. The life I was born into included an absent father and a mother so emotionally and physically abusive that I barely survived. My mother was riddled with undiagnosed conditions such as PTSD, bipolar disorder, and a mood disorder, which made my childhood chaotic and unstable at even the best of times.

I was beaten without explanation, put down, ridiculed, mocked, and made to feel less than human. I was responsible for the care of my siblings and cleanliness of the house from a very young age. My innocence and opportunity to be a carefree child were stolen from me, and I knew mostly pain, fear, and shame during the years I was raised by my mother. There were many times I wanted another life, but somehow, through God, I was able to survive my childhood and thrive in adulthood.

My hope in writing this book is to show people that they can overcome their upbringing. I believe that you can escape the cycle of abuse you were born into. I vowed that I would not be the mother mine was and that I would raise my three girls the way I had wanted to be raised. I loved them, believed in them, and told them often that they could accomplish anything they set their minds to. Thankfully, I succeeded at that. I now have three strong, successful, and beautiful daughters.

You must decide what you want and trust that you do not have to be a product of your past. You can decide to treat people the way you wish your abuser treated you. You can learn to forgive your abuser and lead a happy and healthy life through the decisions you make. You can overcome. You can become all God intended you to be. Your past does not have to define you.

Allow God to use the experiences in your life for your good. That is what God intends to do. Let go and let God do that for you.

They say life is a journey, not a destination, and I believe we should all embrace and enjoy the journey. Consider this your invitation to join me on this adventure and possibly learn a few things along the way. Within the pages of this book is my story, and woven throughout the chapters are lessons in love, strength, resilience, and hope that I pray you will carry with you from this day on. The tears of my past have watered the seeds of my present, and I know that yours can do the same.

Judy

1

It was a beautiful, sunny, cloudless afternoon, and I smiled to myself as the sun warmed my back. The smell of fresh mud surrounded me, and I breathed it in deeply as I squished it through my chubby fingers. I pulled down an old silver pan hanging from the back of the chicken coop and filled it with fresh dirt. I carefully measured out the perfect amount of water from the hydrant and slowly poured it into the pan. I lifted the pan onto my makeshift table and began stirring the mixture together, beaming at the perfect consistency.

There, that should do it, I thought to myself. Without thinking, I wiped my hands on my dress and froze. Fear gripped my chest as I slowly looked down to survey the damage and gasped when I saw two muddy handprints on my freshly cleaned dress.

"She's going to kill me." Beads of sweat gathered on my forehead as I imagined the beating that would no doubt come from this transgression. I never knew which version of my mother I would run into. The happy, forgiving one? Or the one who would beat me senseless for causing her extra work?

My eyes darted from side to side as I sprinted back to the house. My heart spluttered in my chest, and I stilled in the hallway, waiting for any sounds of danger. Satisfied that the coast was clear, I tiptoed to my room and gently closed the door behind me. My breath was coming in ragged gasps as I whipped off my dress and shoved it into my drawer under the rest of them. I hurriedly put on a clean dress and felt myself relax for the first time in several minutes. A giggle escaped my lips, and I skipped all the way back to the mud. Those pies weren't going to make themselves.

It hadn't always been that way. Once upon a time, my mother was kind and caring, but nothing lasts forever, I suppose. Growing up in that house was chaotic at best, terrifying and unsafe at worst. I learned from an early age to mind myself and stay small. If you're small and invisible, you don't get beaten as often. That's what I believed, though the reality was much different.

My mother and siblings believed that I was my daddy's favorite, and for that offense, I was severely ostracized and punished. The jealousy it caused between me and my siblings was unnecessary and painful.

My mother was cruel in her care for me. Though she kept me alive, she took pleasure in my pain. A boy in my class told me there was no Santa Claus, and devastated, I went home crying to my mother for her reassurance that he was lying. Instead of relieving my fears, she chose to crush me instead.

"He's right. There is no Santa Claus," the coldness of her voice sent a chill through my little second grade body.

I was crushed. From then on, there was never anything for me under the Christmas tree. My mother seemed to be thrilled that I knew there was no Santa Claus so that she wouldn't have to buy me anything. She acted as though it shouldn't hurt me, but she knew it did. She loved to hurt me.

Any time there was something I loved or something that made me feel worthy, she was sure to take it from me. I loved my long hair, and she knew it. Much to my horror, she told me that she was going to cut it off. I cried and cried and begged her not to cut it. Instead of consoling me, she slapped me and then cut my hair as short as a boy's. I was humiliated and felt worthless and ugly.

AND THAT'S when my mother decided I was fat. At ten years old, I was wearing a size nine shoe and weighing in at 126 pounds, and she decided I was just too big.

"Judy, you can't wear that; you are too fat," she'd mutter with contempt.

I would retreat to my room, look in the mirror, and repeat her words.

"You are a fat, ugly little girl; who could ever love you?"

Over and over, I would say those words to myself, and I carried that shame for decades.

When I was twelve, my mother decided that I was going on a diet. As an adult, I can see how I was at a perfectly acceptable weight, but as a child, I believed her. We all believe our parents at that age, don't we? I felt I could do nothing right, even with straight A grades in school, and berated myself often.

My "diet" consisted of a piece of meat and a piece of bread. My mother would then make me get on the bicycle and ride up in our pasture for exercise. I've blocked out how long she made me do that for, and the damage was done. It sparked the beginning of a lifelong battle with food, weight, and self-worth.

I was a prisoner in my own house, and it was miserable. Everything about my life was controlled from what time I got up to what time I went to bed to what I watched on TV to what I wore to school to what I ate. Everything was heavily controlled. And yet, I was responsible for so much at the same time.

Once my grandmother moved out and my mother no longer had anyone to answer to, the house began to crumble. The dishes piled up, the once-gleaming floor dulled and filled with clutter, and basic tasks started going undone. Certain that it would be the thing that pleased my mother, I began to do all of the cooking and cleaning.

She hardly noticed.

Some days — unprovoked — she would beat me so badly I could hardly move. I stopped asking what I had done to deserve it. My sin was existing, and there was nothing I could do about that. I learned to simply take my beatings like a good little girl. I didn't fight back. I didn't struggle. What would have been the point? If only someone could have stepped in to save me. But there would be no rescue attempt for me. Even my own father was unable to help. I was completely and utterly alone.

I share all of this not to vilify my mother but to explain the hopelessness I felt as a child, the truth of what I experienced, and to demonstrate the depth of the emotional hole I had to crawl out of. And yet, none of what I went through defines me. I not only survived but thrived later in life. I have kids of my own, and we are incredibly close. I'm living proof that someone can grow up in hell and walk out with buckets of water to help extinguish the pain of others. That's what this book is for.

2

My daddy worked maintenance at school and at a local low-rent housing place. He was a laborer, which just meant he did all the dirty work no one else wanted to do. He dug ditches, crawled underneath houses, and whatever other menial job needed to be done. He wanted better for his six children. His dream for them was a better life than he had. Sadly, that meant he was never at home. I'm not sure if he was unaware of the torture I endured at the hands of my mother or if he felt it was just easier to ignore it. Either way, he was not there to protect me, and that told my fragile little heart that I was all alone.

When I was young, he drove a big yellow school bus, and playing in it before school was one of the rare times I was able to spend time with him. I couldn't wait to start school so I could ride in the big yellow bus. My mother had instilled the fear of God in me when it came to my dad, so I was always afraid of bothering him. "You kids be quiet; your dad is taking a nap." The message from my mother was loud and clear. I had better be quiet, or I was going to get in trouble. I wasn't quite sure if the spanking would come from my mother or my daddy; I just knew I was scared, and I was very careful about being perfect.

Though he seemed supportive of my dreams, even going so far as to buy me a tennis racket when it turned out I was gifted at the sport, he was extremely overprotective. I was gifted in tennis but wasn't allowed to join the team. I was responsible but wasn't allowed to go down the street to have a Coke with a friend. He introduced me to the math team I joined and yet didn't like when I went to meets. It was confusing, and the message that seemed to solidify in my heart was that I was a bother.

I wanted to be popular. I wanted to be a cheerleader, but under my dad's thumb, that was never going to happen. I was only allowed to do things that kept me under his watchful eye. It's ironic, really, when you think about it. He was so worried about me falling in with the wrong crowd or getting hurt outside of the home. What he should have been worried about was what was happening under his own roof. My daddy was overprotective, yes, but not where it mattered — not where I needed him to be. I needed him to protect me from my mother, not from the pep squad.

My dad wanted the best for his kids, and because of that, college wasn't negotiable; we were going. Maybe that was his way of protecting me in the end. Maybe he did know what was happening but couldn't do anything about it. Either way, college is where I found freedom. College is where everything changed for me, and I truly found myself. I stayed away from home as much as I could once I got away. I could always come up with a reason to stay on campus during holidays.

At Thanksgiving, there wasn't going to be anyone on

campus, so I went home. That first night, my dad stayed up with me until 2 a.m., just talking. I had never known my dad before that night. I had never known how much he loved me, how much he really cared for me, how proud he was of me. But that night, my eyes were opened, and the love I felt for him was all-encompassing. Thanks to that night, I knew that everything my mother had told me about my dad was not true. That night changed my life forever. From then on, I knew he was my cheerleader, and he absolutely cheered me on for the rest of his life.

Looking back as an adult, I can see so many moments where my dad did little things that demonstrated his love for me. I couldn't see it in the moment, of course. All I could see as a child was his absence and overbearing nature. But as an adult, I can see the times he bought me makeup because I worked up the nerve to ask or the times he made sure I'd have a job. I can remember how he made me a deal that if I didn't marry until I graduated from college, he'd buy me a car, and he did. There were so many moments that I missed as a child in the throes of turmoil and terror in my own home.

When he died on August 15th, 1998, I was devastated. My cheerleader was gone, and I was lost without him. Though the grief I felt at losing one of the most important people in my life was suffocating, I was also comforted. Grief is only present when there has been much loss, and I was only heartbroken because my daddy and I had become so close. I don't believe that would have happened were it not for the transformation I experienced in college.

It's amazing when you can look back on your life and pinpoint the moment that everything changed. It's rare, really. Not a lot of people experience those moments. Mine was incredibly powerful, but I didn't see it for what it was in the moment. Looking back, though, I am overwhelmed at the simplicity of God's goodness. Where my earthly father had failed, God provided someone in his place who would become my greatest teacher, confidant, and closest friend. Where my earthly father failed, God provided Himself.

3

In every great story, there is a hero who saves the day, and there is a guide who shows the hero how to save the day. God has been my guide.

I always knew about God, but it wasn't until I was in the fourth grade that I went from knowing *about* God to just knowing Him. Making my declaration of faith made it real for me. God became my father and my savior.

In college, I was finally free to figure out who I was and who I was supposed to be. It's where I made God the Lord of my life, not just a "savior" I didn't personally know. It's where I developed a sweet and special relationship with Him. I realized there was much more to being a follower than just not doing bad things. There had been no depth to my relationship with Him before. Now, I had to surrender everything to Him. My hopes, dreams, what I wanted to do — I gave it all to Him. College is where I developed a continual dialog with God.

It all started because I was afraid. When you grow up the way I did, you don't exactly develop excellent people skills. It was the first time I had ever been on my own before, and to be honest, it wasn't going well. I was so afraid of everyone. This is when that moment happened that I talked about in the previous chapter — when everything changed. I cried out to God, and He answered me. I told Him how afraid I was of everyone and how I didn't want to be. Instead of just a comforting feeling, I heard Him tell me to begin to look everyone in the eye and say, "hello." I wasn't exactly thrilled with the instructions, but I also wasn't about to disobey. I did exactly what He said to do, and before I knew it, I had befriended the entire school.

I've been asked before how I learned to hear and discern the still, small voice of God. In college is where it started. I just knew that I knew the answers I was receiving were from God. I tested Him when I needed to and asked Him for verses. When I'm sure, I'm sure. When I'm not sure, I ask for a verse.

Not only did I hear the voice of God, but I also OBEYED the word of God. When He told me to look people in the eye, I did, and soon enough, I knew everyone on campus. The audible voice I heard felt normal, even though I had never actually heard it before. What I knew of the character of God at that point was that He was faithful, so I expected to hear His voice, and I did.

That moment was the beginning of a beautiful relationship with my creator that I still treasure today. The space, silence, and freedom of college allowed for me to hear His still, small voice. I was encouraged to give my testimony in front of a church, and I thought that there was no way I could do that. I cried out to God that I couldn't give my testimony publicly, and God answered with Mark 11:24 — "Therefore I tell you, whatever you ask for in prayer, believe that you have received it, and it will be yours." That's when I knew the Bible was a love letter from God to us. God is my father and also my friend. He answered me when I cried out to Him.

After my dad died, I cried for six straight weeks. I wanted to talk to my dad. I visualized my daddy sitting in his black truck on the hill behind my house, getting away from my mother. I could see him drive the truck down to the fence, jump over it, and come and sit and talk to me. We would laugh, and he had such a contagious laugh. He was so fun, and I missed him desperately. I just wanted to talk to him. In a voice as audible as any I have ever heard, I heard God say to me,

"Judy, as much as you long to talk to your dad, I long for you to talk to me."

What? What had I just heard? God longs to talk to me as much as I long to talk to my dad! I couldn't believe it, so I asked, "God, was that really you? You want to talk to me as much as I long to talk to my dad?" How could that be? I was just Judy Taylor; why would God long to talk to me? I said, "God I know that was you, but I want to make sure. Will you please give me a scripture out of the Bible to let me know that was you?"

I got my Bible and just let it fall open, and there it was, the verse God wanted me to read — Isaiah 30:18: "Yet the Lord longs to be gracious to you; he rises to show you compassion. For the Lord is a God of justice. Blessed are all who wait for Him!"

Wow! There was my verse. God does long for me to talk to Him. He rises to show me compassion, and He is the God of justice. I am blessed when I wait for Him. I was so blown away by this interaction between me and God. I had been having a quiet time since I was eighteen, but that changed everything. I was no longer having a quiet time just because I was supposed to. I was not having a quiet time so I could grow. I was not having a quiet time because other ministers had told me it was what I was supposed to do. No, I was having a quiet time because God longed for me to talk to him. He was waiting every morning for me to come and meet with him. He loved me and wanted to know about my day. God changed my life once again.

Asking God for help, listening for the answer, acting in faith based on what you hear —that is how you begin to transform your life. Regardless of what we grew up experiencing, we can always make room for the voice of God. God is waiting to intervene and to talk to us if only we would ask.

4

Though as a child, I didn't know God the way I do now, I believe that He sent special gifts to me so that I wouldn't break. One of those gifts was music.

My mother had always dreamed that we would be a family centered around music. She wanted us to play the piano and sing together. In the spring of my third grade year, she bought an old upright piano from a family friend for $50. That summer, I started taking lessons from someone my dad knew, and I loved it.

The house was full at that time with four kids, and my mother went into rages often. She would scream and yell at me for no reason, and the way her face turned red with anger made me so afraid of her. I believed that I could do nothing right, and I had zero self-esteem. My mother was such an angry woman, and to escalate the situation, she was pregnant again.

My dad was working three jobs to put beans and potatoes on the table, so I was in the house with a ticking time bomb. I had no one to show me love. What I realized as an adult was that she was actually angry with my dad for never being around. He thought he was doing the right thing by working morning, noon, and night, but it left us both feeling abandoned by him.

Practicing the piano seemed to help my mother's mood, so I would sit on the piano bench and play, and the notes on the page were easy for me to remember. I really don't know if the reason I loved to play was because I was good at it or because I could bang on those notes and let out all of my anger. Either way, it was an escape for me. When there was too much chaos in the house, I would go practice, and it would calm me down.

That old upright piano served me well, especially on the days my mother was on the warpath. Looking back over this period of my life, I know God was there. God had my mother buy that old upright piano just for me because He knew it would save me. God knew I would be talented in music, and it would be a way that I could feel Him in my life. I would know that God was with me.

My mother sent me off to church with my aunt who lived across the street, and I started going to Sunday school. I remember entering that Sunday school class and finding out that my much-older cousin had told them I could play the piano, so I was recruited that very day to play for an assembly at the church. The teacher picked out a hymn, and I was terrible. I can still hear the high school boys laughing at me. I could have given up, but I was determined to learn, and I did.

Two years later, the pianist of the church had a sick husband and was no longer able to attend, so I was asked to fill in. My Sunday school teacher told me that I couldn't be the main pianist unless I made a profession of faith, joined the church, and was baptized. My mother had told me that I was the age of accountability two years prior, which basically meant that I was lost and in need of saving by Jesus. I had wanted to give my heart to Him and make a public profession of my faith, but I was so shy and scared that I couldn't. The teacher told me that I had enough strength to walk down the aisle and give my heart and life to Jesus Christ, so I did.

I felt like I was floating on air for months. Jesus Christ lived in my heart, and I knew He loved me so very much. I became the pianist for the big church, and music proved to be a comfort to me that weaved throughout my life. Here again, God showed up in my life to show me how much He loved me and how I could be of service and feel loved by Him.

I continued to be the pianist of the church until I graduated from high school. At some point, I found the hymns so boring that I started playing around with different runs to spice up my playing. Again, I know this was God saying, "Judy, come on, let's change things up a bit; let's make this fun," and oh, was it ever fun!

Before I left for college, my mother told me she wanted me to take private piano lessons. She had such a hold on me that I felt I had to do what she told me to do. I trotted right over to the music department housed in the lower part of the chapel and announced that I was there to sign up for private piano lessons. The professors all laughed at me and told me that I could not sign up for private piano lessons unless I declared a major or minor in music. This was actually perfect for me because I knew in the first grade that I was going to be a teacher, and as I grew older, I was good at math, so I knew I wanted to teach math. Secondary education required two subjects, and that was what my major actually was — secondary education math and music. When I finished my degree, I would be able to teach math or music from sixth through 12th grade. It was the last major decision I allowed my mother to make for me.

These are the memories I look back on and see God in and through. Even though my mother was hateful and abusive, her love of music became a safe haven to me. Music was where I could escape, get my frustrations out, and feel safe for a time. Music was a tool that God used in my life, and I am so grateful.

5

There were many times in my childhood that I felt less than. Though I loved school, the other children seemed to have much more than I did. I had to wait for the bus every day, so I was left in the classroom with my teacher, Mrs. Henderson. All of the other kids' mothers would pick them up. The rest of the kids had such beautiful pencil boxes, crayons, and pens. I longed for beautiful things because I did not have any. I had no crayons or pictures to color at home.

When Christmas time rolled around my mother decided that we would go visit her parents on Christmas Eve, which meant that Santa Claus would come (I hadn't been told he wasn't real yet). I will never forget coming through the door and seeing the house lit only by the warm glow of the Christmas tree. As the lights flickered and danced in my vision, there she was. My breath caught, and I stopped dead in my tracks as my eyes fell upon the most beautiful doll I had ever seen sitting underneath the tree waiting for me. It was the most magical time of my entire life. Honestly, I have been trying to feel that same feeling ever since.

The following Christmas was the year I was told there was no Santa Claus and I was devastated. I didn't get anything for Christmas that year, and the following years, I received nothing except for hair brushes, pantyhose, and other nonsense.

When I was ten years old, and in the fourth grade, my mother had this bright idea that it would make me feel better if I played Santa for my younger siblings. It didn't. I was so depressed because there was nothing under the tree for me. I continued to long for that feeling of awe I experienced when I was seven. When I was in the fifth grade, she gave my older sister and I each a birthstone ring. It was not what I wanted, so I didn't appreciate it at all. I felt so left out, and things did not improve as I got older. As I returned to school after the holidays each year, my classmates would share with enthusiasm about all the wonderful gifts they received. They would turn to me with expectancy, and my shoulders would droop as I was made to admit year after year that there had been nothing under the tree for me.

Even now, I still look for that feeling of awe at Christmas. Don't get me wrong, I love Christmas because I love to give gifts to my children and grandchildren, but I have continued to experience that feeling of being left out. It is not that I want gifts; I just want that incredible feeling of awe.

While writing this, I was asked to start going through the book, *The Artist's Way*. One of the assignments in that book is that I am to take myself out for an artist date every week. My very first artist's date resulted in me feeling that awe I have been searching for since I was seven years old. I know God led me to do this. My God is a God of restoration.

You see, I asked God to show me what I should do for my first artist's date. I did not want to go very far, and I didn't want to spend much money. God led me to go to the local Dollar General and get a color-by-number picture and two Sprite zeros and then go to the local park across the street from the Methodist church. As soon as I sat down and began to color, I felt the awe and excitement I felt when I was seven, even though I was now sixty-eight! After all this time, all I had needed to do was nurture the little girl inside me. I simply needed to do fun stuff with her the way I wished my mother had done. I realized that I can be the mom of my little seven-year-old Judy.

I went back to the store to get a frame for my color-by-number. I also bought little Judy a small backpack with beautiful crayons, a pencil holder, and a zipped bag to keep beautiful things in — exactly what I had wanted when I was a child but never received. I went home and displayed my color-by-number on my kitchen table for everyone to see.

That day, God healed a wound that had been buried deep in my heart for more than sixty years. We can't go back and change the past. The things that happened were awful, and there's no sense denying that. But God, in His infinite wisdom and grace, can heal even the deepest of wounds decades later. Time does not heal all wounds, but God can. If there are scars you've been holding onto, perhaps it's time to relinquish their hold on you and let the God of restoration restore what has been stolen from you.

6

Going to college was the thrill of my life, and it's where I really learned to trust the voice of God.

We loaded up the trunk of my car with everything I owned and drove an hour to the place that I would call home for the next four years. As we drove into the entrance of the college, I was so full of excitement, wonder, and terror. My family helped me unload the car, we said our goodbyes, and they drove off. I was already feeling the freedom of being on my own, and it was something I had longed for my entire life.

I spent a lot of time on our college courtyard we called the quad just talking to people and getting to know them. It was great fun, and that is something I had really never experienced — having fun. I loved getting to know people, where they were from, what they were majoring in, and about their families. This was just a few weeks into the fall of my freshman year, and I was coming into myself. I had studied my entire life, and now, I didn't even want to study; I just wanted to be around loving people.

We had a spiritual emphasis week during that fall, and

the guy that played Eb on Green Acres was our speaker. He spoke of making God Lord of your life, and I had never heard of that concept. I thought I was a good little Christian girl because I didn't smoke, drink, swear, have sex, or hang around anybody that did. I was in for a rude awakening. Making God the Lord of my life was eye opening for me. I had always wanted to grow as a Christian during my teenage years but just didn't know how. Make God Lord of my life, surrender all to him, die daily to myself — I would pray that prayer every day for the next forty years but truly not understand what it meant. I was very sincere in my prayers, but I did not understand them until many years later.

Don't read the Bible just because you are supposed to, but read it because it is a love letter to you from God. God loves me more than I could imagine. Wow, what a revelation! All I had ever known from my church was that I was a filthy dirty sinner in need of a Savior and my mother telling me how fat and ugly I was. Now, it seemed I was hearing the truth for the very first time in my life. I am a sinner saved by grace. I am covered by His blood, and now, I am white as snow. I am a new creation completely loved by God because of what Jesus has done just for me.

I started reading my Bible through those eyes. This book is a love letter to me from God. I started reading in Romans, and it really spoke to me. Every day, I was growing more and more as a Christian, and all the while, Jesus was leading the way. In the Bible, the book of Romans says, "who can separate us from the love of Christ?" Nothing can separate us from the love of Christ. "We are more than conquerors through Him who loved us."

It seemed everybody on campus was going to be a missionary, and I was so afraid that God was going to call me to be a missionary to deep, dark Africa. "Oh, God, I don't want to do that," I would say. It took me until my sophomore year to have the courage to say, "Okay, God, whatever you want me to do, I will do it. If deep, dark Africa is where you want me to go, I will." God answered, "Judy, being a missionary in deep, dark Africa is not what I have for you, but I wanted you to be willing to do that if that is what I wanted you to do." What a lesson!

After Christmas, I returned to college for the spring semester. Little did I know, this semester would change my life in so many wonderful ways. There was an organization on campus called the Baptist Student Union (BSU). They had a paper drive at the local projects. There were lots of little kids, and they seemed to gravitate to me. The president of the BSU noticed it and asked me if I would serve on the council as the missions coordinator. I was so honored and surprised, and I accepted the challenge. The major outreach we did was to go to the projects in town, put all the kids on a bus, take them to a church, and basically have Vacation Bible School with them every Saturday morning. I loved my time serving on the BSU council.

Another mission opportunity I had was spring break missions. We went to an area of need, and during the week, we did youth-led revivals. Each team had four members — preacher, music director, pianist, and fellowship director. We were sent to an encampment where we cleared brush and made a prayer garden at the top of a mountain.

Working with men made me feel uneasy because my mother had always been afraid that her kids would be taken, and so she told us terrible things about them. Because of that, I was scared of everyone to some extent but especially of young men. I learned that week how special it was for young men and women to work side by side for a cause. If it had not been for the healing I received that week,

I might have been too frightened to ever get married, and I would have missed the most wonderful thing that has ever happened to me. God healed me so much that week in so many ways.

I was informed that the church we would serve wanted us to come early and get to know the people and give our testimony. We were to visit two Sundays before we actually did the youth-led revival. The first visit, when I first found out we would have to give a testimony, I was sitting beside the music director, and I said, "I cannot do this." I was so scared. She wrote on her bulletin, "You're right, Judy; you can't, but God can."

I went back to the dorm and started crying out to God; I needed His help. In the next few days, God gave me scriptures that meant so much to me. The first scripture was Mark 11:24, "Therefore, I say unto you, What things soever ye desire, when ye pray, believe that you receive them, and ye shall have them."

"Oh, thank you, God, I am so scared to do this testimony; please help me." This was the first of several scriptures He gave me. Next was 1 John 5:14-15, "And this is the confidence that we have in him, that, if we ask anything according to his will, he hears us, and if we know that he hears us, whatsoever we ask, we know that we have the petitions that we desired of him."

Wow, so if I ask and believe, He will give me what I ask for. I needed confidence, and there was the scripture that said that I could have confidence in God. Then, God gave me 2 Timothy 1:7, "For God hath not given us the spirit of fear; but of power, and of love, and of a sound mind."

He gave me three scriptures within a few days after I cried out to Him, and those scriptures meant so much to me that I was able to get in front of that church and give my testimony. The way God revealed Himself to me through that experience absolutely changed the way I looked at Him.

I was like a tight little rosebud that had not opened yet. Each day, that rose opened a little more until I blossomed into a fully opened flower. College transformed my life. I stopped being afraid of people, I was no longer terrified to get in front of people, and I was in leadership positions in the BSU and Student Government. I continued to grow in the Lord, I kept making great friends, and I continued to pursue my goal of finishing my education and become a fantastic teacher. I was not the same person. In fact, I had one of my classmates from high school tell me just that. "Judy, you went off to school and came back a totally different person." That was definitely a complement.

Every summer, I stayed at school and took classes because I just could not stand being at home for three months with my mother. I remember that first summer when I was still nineteen, I was walking across campus, and I could hear God whispering to me. I thought, "God, is that you?" Of course, it was, and I began dialoging with God constantly. The verse that says "pray continually" doesn't mean you have to be all alone on your knees. I learned that God could be talking to me, and I could be talking to Him ALL the time. Wow, that was amazing to me.

Another big moment was when I realized God had answered my prayer in a huge way. When I was thirteen or fourteen, I prayed that God would give me a new family, new town, friends, and make me popular. God did that! When I went off to college, I got a new family, new town, new friends, and I was popular. My God did all that for me, and I would not have realized that if I had not written this book. Our God is an awesome God. He cares about the little things in our lives that are such big things to us. He hears and answers our requests, and sometimes, we don't see them because we are not looking for them. Ask and you shall receive them. Ask Him to open your eyes to see how He is working in your life.

All these years, I had thought my healing did not start until I was thirty-three but through the writing of this book, I realized that my healing started the day my dad left me at the doorstep of my dorm. I was free, and my healing had begun.

"Oh, God, thank you so much for opening my eyes to see what you have done throughout my life. It is truly a miracle. Thank you for leading and guiding me. Thank you for your still small voice. Thank you for always whispering to me which way to go next, and thank you for leading me to make the right choice."

They were all choices that I made, but God led me, and I chose to follow.

7

M any little girls dream of their wedding and plan every detail of that glorious day. They dream of what their fiancés will be like and the life that they will make together. This is a dream I never had growing up. I was convinced that no one would ever love me like that, and there would be no marriage or children in my future.

I can remember being on the pep squad bus headed to a Friday night football game, and they would sing this silly song where they would say the girl's name and who her boyfriend was. Oh, how I wanted to be one of those girls that had a boyfriend. I longed to be cared for by someone, and I thought a boyfriend would do that for me.

My freedom came when I went off to college, but I still had a lot to learn before I would meet my future husband. I did want to finish school before I got married, so I asked God not to let me meet who I was to marry until I had finished my education. I never even had a close call.

My older sister preceded me to that same small Christian school three years before, met a young man the fall of her freshman year, fell in love, and quit school. This prompted my father's bribe that if I finished school before I got married, he would buy me a car. I told him he'd better start saving his pennies, nickels, and dimes because this girl was finishing school before she got married.

I dated a little during the first three and a half years of college but nothing serious. I was beginning to feel very lonely. At one point, I asked God if there was something wrong with me, and He was so gracious to remind me that I had asked to not meet my future husband until I had finished school. I met my husband in March of my senior year, just two months before finishing school. We almost passed in the night, but God's timing is always perfect. He was a freshman, and I was a senior. There was no way I could have met him until then because he was still in high school. I am glad my loneliness did not get the best of me. I waited for the best, and he is absolutely the love of my life even after forty-five years of marriage.

I decided I did not want to go home after I graduated from college, so I had to come up with a plan. My dad would have made me come home to live if I wasn't married because he was old school. You lived at home until you married. In his eyes, it was not proper for a young woman to live alone. I knew I couldn't go back there, so I had to do something. With the connections I had with the BSU, there were ways I could serve after graduating from college and not have to go back home. I applied for the campus evangelism coordinator position at West Texas State University, and I got the job. I was so excited about the possibilities for ministry. That solved the problem of having to return home after graduating from college, but I still felt alone.

One fall weekend during my senior year, I was so lonely that I did not want to spend the weekend in my room. I went over to the recreation building and played a game of foosball with a couple and another friend. I barely remember it, but later, my husband helped me remember that it was him I had been playing foosball against.

I had a female friend that I ran around with, and one night, we went to McDonald's to get something to eat. While we were sitting eating our dinner, one of the boys she knew from the intramural softball team came in to eat, and because he knew her, he sat down with us. Little did I know that he was the chosen one for me, he would become my beloved, and God had chosen the perfect man for me.

We started hanging out together. We would load up in someone's car and go to the dollar movie, McDonald's, or the park to swing on the swings. It was great fun. I still had no idea that there was anything but friendship between us. He was a freshman, and I was a senior. He was three years younger than I was.

This went on for a couple of months. It was April, my junior/senior banquet was coming up, and I did not want to go by myself, so I started looking for a male friend to accompany me. I am certain it was a God thing because I decided to ask David, and he accepted. I was still thinking it was just a friendship thing. After the junior/senior banquet, we were inseparable.

He told me later that in May, he went back to his high school and talked to a teacher that he was very close to. David told him that he had met a girl that he was interested in but didn't have anything to fall back on, and his teacher said that if you really love her, half the fun of it is making it together. He encouraged him to go for it.

Of course, I was in summer school because I was not going home for any length of time, and David would visit me at school. One night in July, we had gone to the local park, and he said, "What do you think about us getting married?"

I replied, "Well, a girl likes to be asked," and he said, "I am asking." I said yes, and I let him get away with that proposal.

I was heading off to West Texas State because I had already made that commitment and it was definitely a God thing. David and I had only known each other for five months. We really did not know each other at all. So for the next nine months, we wrote to each other every day and took turns calling on the weekend. We did not have cell phones in 1976, and the phone bill was outrageous. I put my letters from him in a box, and he put his letters from me in a box, and we still have those two boxes of letters. We got to know each other by the written word that year.

Over the years, I have read many books on relationships, and one of the books I read had you consider why you were attracted to your spouse. I thought about that, and when I first met David, I had girls in my room all the time to talk to me about their problems, but none of them listened to *me*. I needed someone to listen to me, and when I first met David, that is all we did. I talked, and he listened. He was so very quiet.

After forty-five years, I talk, and he still listens. God has also shown me that growing up with someone like my mother, I needed someone who would always support me. David would never say anything hurtful to me or about me. He is always there for me. He always encourages me to do what I feel I need to. He has loved me whether I weighed 276 pounds or 176 pounds. He is the love of my life, and I know that he was another prayer answered by my God who would never forsake me.

8

Growing up with as much dysfunction as I did is going to manifest in different ways for different people. For me, it was through my weight. My mother had convinced me at a young age that I was fat and ugly, and with that came the belief that I was also unworthy.

I went off to college weighing about 180 pounds. I maintained that weight until I got married and started having children. The funny thing about those years though, was that I continued to tell myself I was fat and ugly, even though I was far from it. I had not yet learned the truth, and I believed the lies spoken to me by my mother.

I started journaling when I was eighteen and I can look back at the words I wrote and just cry.

"Oh God, please can't you help me just eat normally? I know you are not happy with me because I am so fat."

Lie! Lie! Lie! The truth is that I was fearfully and wonderfully made in the image of God, and I am beautiful in His sight, but I would not let myself believe that. For years, I loathed my body and my weight. I could not stand to look in the mirror because I thought I was so ugly.

I gained 62 pounds with my first child and got up to 232 pounds. At that point, the loathing took on a new dimension. I loved my baby so much, and I was so happy to be a mom, especially since my own mother had me convinced no one would ever love me. It was a dream come true that I was married and had a precious baby girl, but I would look in the mirror and think, "Judy, you are fat and ugly." I managed to get most of the baby weight off, and then I was pregnant again and gained about fifty pounds. Then, I was pregnant again and had my third baby in October of 1983. I did not gain very much weight with this baby, and I was at a reasonable weight for a very short period of time.

As the years went by, my self-loathing did not improve, and I continued to gain weight. I would go for days without eating and lose twenty pounds only to gain that back and more. They call it yo-yo dieting, and I was the queen of it.

When I was thirty-five I decided to go to a diet center to help me lose weight. On that diet, I could hardly eat anything and had to take a bunch of supplements. I went in weighing 224 pounds, and a short four and a half months later, I weighed 153 pounds. At five feet, ten inches and a huge frame, I was skin and bones, and I loved it, but it wasn't long until I was gaining it back. When I reached 170 pounds, my husband said, "Please don't ever get that small again; I felt like I was hugging bones." What a wonderful husband. I had lost the weight quickly but gained it back just as fast.

That was 1990, and by 1996, I weighed in at a whopping 276 pounds, which was the most I had ever weighed. All those years, I journaled and asked God to just let me eat normally and lose the weight, but it never happened. I looked in the yellow pages and found another weight loss program, and again, I did exactly as I was told — because I was a people pleaser — and I lost 100 pounds in about seven months. I looked great at 176 pounds, but again, that diet was very restrictive, and I grew tired of eating chicken, fish, or salad for every meal. Fish for breakfast is just not appetizing to me. I stopped that program and did not go through maintenance to teach me how to add foods back in, and it wasn't long before I was gaining again.

For the next seventeen years, I would gain weight, get back on that program, lose 30 pounds, stop going, and then gain weight again and repeat the process. I kept this up until I was sixty. Eventually, I thought, "This is the definition of insanity — doing the same thing over and over expecting a different result. I am paying for this program every month to starve me to death, something I cannot maintain, and I lose and then gain it right back. I am not doing this anymore."

God said something truly profound to me once I surrendered.

"Judy, if you don't love yourself at 276 pounds, you will not love yourself at 153 pounds. It is a number. I want you to love yourself just as you are — the way I love you."

So I started looking in the mirror and telling myself that I was beautiful, and all my curves were beautiful. All the while, my husband totally and completely loved me. He did not care what I weighed; he loved me — just like God did.

Every morning and throughout the day, I made myself look in the mirror and told myself, "You are beautiful." It was so very hard for me to do that because I believed the lie that I was fat and ugly, but I would repeat, "No, you are not fat and ugly; you are beautiful," over and over again. I told myself I was beautiful every day.

God had already told me that I would never love myself at 175 pounds if I didn't love myself at 275 pounds, and I believed Him. I had been on enough diets. I had read every book on the market on eating properly. I had read every book there was on dieting. I knew all the fad diets out there and had done them all with the exception of diet pills. I knew what was good for me to eat, and I knew that I needed to eat; that definitely was not the problem. The problem was that I was living to eat instead of eating to live.

I ate when I was happy, when I was sad, when I was mad, when I was bored, when I was scared, when I felt any emotion at all. I was stuffing my feelings. Then, I would turn around and eat nothing. It was a vicious cycle, and I was so tired of it.

When I was sixty I decided to get off the roller coaster ride of yo-yo dieting. I looked in the mirror and fell in love with my big beautiful body and started dressing that body. I actually felt very good about myself. I honestly knew I was beautiful. During that time, I was eating properly. I didn't eat processed food most of the time. I ate good fruits and vegetables and lean meat, and I kept my calorie intake between 1000 and 1800 calories a day. I felt I should have been losing weight, but I didn't. I just kept looking in the mirror and telling myself that I was beautiful.

I still question why I didn't lose weight. I have asked several doctors, and they don't know either. All I know is that God led me to love myself first. I won't lie, I did not like weighing 258 pounds. That is what I had weighed off and on for 20 years, but I do know God was telling me I had to love myself at that weight before I could love myself at any other weight.

In October of 2019, when I was sixty-six I had been feeling really bad, so I made an appointment with my doctor. She informed me that my A1C was eight, and I was diabetic. She put me on 1000 mg of Metformin twice a day, and the weight started dropping off. I did not change my eating habits. Within the first year, I had lost twenty pounds, and by the end of the second year, I had lost another twenty pounds.

In December of 2021, I knew I needed to exercise to help me with the diabetes. I knew I could not motivate myself, so I searched for personal trainers in my area. I couldn't afford to actually hire a personal trainer, but I was hoping for some help. I found an app called Kickoff. I filled out the information they wanted, and luckily, Teresa, my trainer, texted me the next day with all the information, and it was something I could afford. I committed to working out for thirty minutes a day, and as of writing this, I will have worked out every day for 585 days and have run two 10k runs!

I went back to the doctor for a checkup in March, and I actually weighed 204 pounds and had an A1C of 5.6. The doctor was thrilled and took me off the medication. Hallelujah, I didn't have to take Metformin any longer. I had another checkup with her six months later, and she said I was maintaining my diabetes with diet and exercise.

Is this still a struggle? Absolutely. Do I work at it? Every day. Do I look in the mirror and loathe myself? Not anymore. Do I eat ice cream? If I want some. My best advice to people who are not comfortable in their own skin and are not happy with their weight is that you have to love yourself first, get on an eating plan that you can live with for the rest of your life, tell yourself you are beautiful multiple times a day, exercise every day even if it is just for ten minutes, relax, and accept yourself the way you are. God made you just like you are, and you are beautiful.

Some of the best advice I have run across is the 80/20 plan. This means you eat clean eighty percent of the time and eat whatever you want twenty percent of the time. For those who need a little more explanation, if you eat three meals a day, that is twenty one meals a week. For four of those meals, you'll eat anything you want to eat and then get back on your clean eating plan. That means for seventeen of your meals a week, you are eating fruits, vegetables, meat, fish, and whole grains.

You can also pick whatever plan you want to eat; just stick with it. If you didn't lose weight this week, don't have an all-or-nothing mentality like I did. Stay on your plan for the long haul; eventually, it will happen. Plan your work, and work your plan. You can do it, and don't forget, there is no eating plan that is going to solve your problem. The problem is that if you don't value yourself, you do not see your beauty, and you do not accept yourself for the beautiful person you are. That's understandable if you've experienced the kind of childhood I have. Look in that mirror and tell yourself you are beautiful, made in God's image, and God accepts you for exactly the way you are. You also need to accept yourself exactly the way you are. If you love yourself and accept that you are the temple of God, everything else will fall into place.

9

After years of my mother's verbal, emotional, and physical abuse, by the time I was eighteen, I'd had all I could take. "I will never let anyone hurt me again." It was a vow I made from a place of self-protection. I was the daughter that did her best to be perfect. I was the one who took care of the kids, cleaned the house, had dinner on the table when she came home from work, and took the kids to church. I was the one who did everything she told me to do, but it was never enough. If my own mother could not love me well, I knew I would need to make sure no one had the power to hurt me.

No more emotions for Judy. No pain, no hurt feelings, no feelings of joy, nothing. I simply existed. I lived that way for fifteen years.

During my college years, I felt the freedom of not being at home, so I felt happy all the time. I had fallen in love with people and thought they were perfect. I loved being around people, so the only emotion I felt was sheer happiness. No one ever hurt my feelings because there were no feelings to hurt. Nothing I experienced ever compared to the hell I lived in growing up so, in comparison, life was great.

After my engagement with David, I went off to West Texas State for the year. David would come and visit periodically, and when it was time for him to leave, he would be the one crying and not me. That should have told me something right there. I was clueless that anything was wrong. I simply didn't cry. I knew I would miss him, but there was absolutely no deep feeling of loss for him not being there.

When I was planning our wedding, no one helped me. I made all the plans. There was a local store where I found my dress. It was white eyelet for $220, and I wore a hat. I gathered up all my bridesmaids and maid of honor, found a little bakery in town that would make a very inexpensive cake for around $50, and got just enough flowers for the bridesmaids and David's best men for about $130. I did not want my mother involved at all because she would have taken over and done it her way.

My wedding cost me about $500, and I paid for it myself. When I got home, my mother decided that she absolutely had to do something, so she went down to the flower shop and ordered an arch for us to stand under with flowers all over it.

I still had no feelings whatsoever. I could feel the wall all around me. My maid of honor, the girl who played on the softball team with David, did not show up for my wedding. Even that didn't hurt my feelings. Who does that? Have no feelings, I mean. Any other girl would have been hysterical. Not me. I had made bridesmaid dresses for all my sisters and David's sister, so she just filled in for the maid of honor. My dad walked me down the aisle and leaned over and said, "You know, it is not too late to back out." I looked straight at David and pulled my dad down the aisle. My future was standing underneath that arch waiting for me, and I was running toward him.

Three years into our marriage, we had our first child, and the plan was for me to stay home with the children. It was my choice. I wanted to raise them myself. Plus, if I was a teacher, I would have had to spend half my salary on child-care. What was the point of working?

When my daughter was a year old, the high school principal called me and said he could not find a math teacher anywhere. Would I consider coming back? My husband and I talked it over and decided it would be helpful since he had just started a new job and was not making very much. One morning, I was taking the baby to the babysitter, and I saw my husband headed to work with a girl in the truck with him. He had not bothered to tell me that he was carpooling with a couple of co-workers and one of them happened to be a girl. Oh, did Satan have a heyday with my emotions and feelings.

I had never been jealous with my husband. I was very secure in his love and knew he loved me completely and I was the only one for him. But there it was; jealousy had reared its ugly head. I was pregnant shortly after, and that jealousy grew and grew. Seven months after my second baby was born, I found out I was pregnant again. With all those emotions going on, that jealousy had taken over my body, mind, and spirit. I can remember going to the window, watching my husband drive away to work, and being consumed by rage. After my third baby was born, I had a come-to-Jesus meeting and said, "Jesus, I cannot live this way anymore. I know my husband loves me, but I cannot shake this jealousy."

Jesus reminded me of what I knew to be true — that if I command Satan to flee in the name of Jesus, he has to go. I wish I could tell you that I commanded Satan to flee one time and that was the end of it, but I was too consumed. One time did not do the trick. I would say, "Get thee behind me Satan" hundreds of times a day. It took thirty days to break the hold Satan had on me, but after thirty days, that jealousy was gone through the power of Jesus Christ, and I have not had a problem with it since. That was forty-two years ago. I was really surprised I had the problem in the first place; I was completely blindsided, but isn't that the way Satan works?

I have always been involved with church work, and so-called Christian people can be the worst. I was a pianist for several churches and there again, though at times people were cruel to me, I never got my feelings hurt. I just didn't care what they thought. I would say, "I feel God leading me to do this, and I don't care what you think." Nothing hurt my feelings.

When I was thirty-three God came to me and said, "Judy, do you think it is normal for you not to feel anything?" When I heard God say that to me, I thought for a second and said, "No, that is not normal." Everyone I knew got their feelings hurt all the time, and as soon as I acknowledged that, it was like that wall I had built just fell to the ground. I felt so exposed, so naked. When I went to church, I felt every emotion, every feeling from the people who were there, and I felt responsible for fixing them. Whew! It was intense. Thankfully, that did not last forever, just for a few months.

After acknowledging that it was not healthy for me to lack feelings, God led me for the next five years in the beginning of my healing. What a journey! I was really afraid to take the journey alone. I was afraid I would just lose my mind or something because of the wall I had built around me. God led me to seek out a Godly woman whom I trusted, and I met with her once a week for about six months to help me talk all this out. God also led me to books that helped me heal. I did not realize until I read these books that when you are emotionally abused, you shut everything down. You are not allowed to feel anything, so you just shut down.

One book was "Adult Children of Abusive Parents" by Steven Farmer. The author had exercises throughout the book to help you get in touch with yourself. They were simple exercises, such as get in a quiet place, listen, and identify what you hear — the refrigerator, your breathing, your heartbeat. Whatever you hear, acknowledge it because that is what you shut down as a child.

In another book, "The Gift of Inner Healing" by Ruth Cater Stapleton, I learned about the healing of memories where basically you sit quietly and remember the most devastating things that happened in your life, and you take Jesus with you. Jesus will hold your hand, and as you remember the awful things that happened to you, Jesus is there to reassure you that He is there and will protect you. After you have remembered these things, Jesus is there to create new memories in the place of the old scary ones. He shows you how it should have been. The people who were supposed to protect you and love you and did not, Jesus is there to say, "I was there, and this is the way this should have played out. When you think of these memories, you now have new memories in their place."

By the time I had met with my trusted friend, read through the books God had led me through, and had done the exercises, about five years had passed. The last exercise in the book "Adult Children of Abusive Parents" the author said to only do when you are ready. It was to imagine your-self on a grassy knoll with the people who had hurt you.

Look at those people. Feel how they hurt you. Know they did do the best they could. When you are ready, approach each person, look them in the eye, say what they did to you, and then forgive them. Oh, what a release! I forgave my mother, knowing she did the best she could.

Although forgiving my mother did make things better, the hurt was still there. She knew how to push my buttons, and she had a way of hurting me over and over. I forgave her again and again, but I also limited the time I spent with her. It was just too painful. I still had work to do. When I was about forty-eight I watched a movie that God used to teach me another lesson. The movie was about a young man who was a genius but had been brutally traumatized by his father, and the young man's counselor said to him over and over that it wasn't his fault. What his dad did to him was not his fault. It was as if God was saying, "Judy, how your mother was is not your fault." My mother being an angry, bitter, old woman is not my fault! I didn't even know I had those feelings. I didn't know I blamed myself for how my mother was, but I can see that it was because she blamed me for her unhappiness. She believed that I was there to make her happy, but no one could do that.

MY MOTHER HAD HURT me so deeply that I could not see my worth. After I had gone through the books of healing, God then led me to think through those things that I felt about myself. God asked me if those feelings were true. The answer was — and is — no. All of those feelings are lies from hell. God then led me to replace them with the truth using this mantra:

I am fearfully and wonderfully made,

I was chosen before the foundation of the earth,

I was chosen by God, God called me by name,

I am His beloved daughter with whom He is well pleased,

I was made in the image of God,

I am beautiful in his sight, and I can wear anything I want because I am so tall.

I would love to tell you that I said that mantra one time and never had to say it again, but that would not be true. Satan is very crafty, and he knows your weaknesses. When you least expect it, he is going to come after you to bring you down so that you cannot be an effective messenger of the Gospel. I had to say this mantra over and over and over all through my forties, fifties, and sixties. The more you say it, the more Satan will leave you alone, but you never reach an end because Satan prowls around like a roaring lion seeking to find someone to devour. Keep your vigil about putting the truth in your mind, and in the name of Jesus, command Satan to leave you alone, and he has to flee.

When I reached fifty, I truly had forgiven my mother, but I knew there was more to it than just forgiving her. I knew that the first eighteen years of my life living with her affected me in ways I could not imagine. I am not a psychologist, but I knew there was more healing to do. So I began to pray that God would help me see what other work needed to be done in my life.

I noticed that God would send people in my life just like my mother. I would say, "God, have I not had enough of this type of personality?" and He would reply, "Dear child, there are still things that you need to learn." I thought I had suffered enough.

What God was teaching me was that there were people who would try to push my buttons, but I didn't have to let them succeed. There was, and is, always a way out. There are times God will lead me to say something, and there are days He tells me to be quiet. Just walk with the Lord, and He will help deal with the difficult people in your life. You do not have to let them push your buttons.

Because my mother never allowed any personal opinions about anything, I was too afraid to confront anyone. One day, I overheard my boss tell a colleague that I would not be good at leadership because I was unorganized. The crazy thing about that was I had already told him I did not want the leadership position. Why didn't he just say that? Well, it was because God wanted to teach me something. I called my sisters, who were both in leadership positions, and my wonderful husband. They all told me that I had to confront him. I told my husband, "I am afraid I will go in there and just cry the entire time." David suggested that I write everything down and just go in and read it.

The very next day, I did ask for a meeting. When I told him I was in my office and overheard his conversation, he just hung his head. We talked for about five minutes, and he apologized. I share this story because I know that God wanted me to learn that if I confront people, I will not die, and neither will you. I am still breathing. After that confrontation, I have not been afraid to confront people when they need to be confronted.

Over the years, I have gotten stronger and stronger. There are people like my mother who show up in my life sent by God to continue to teach me. God is not through with me yet, and there are things I can learn from the effects my mother still has on me from my childhood. I still have feelings that I have to stop and examine and see why I am feeling them in the first place, but once I do, those feelings dissipate in minutes. Where it used to take days, weeks, or months to get over some feeling I was experiencing, it now takes minutes, hours, or a day. I have to stop, feel the feeling, call it what it is, and it seems to lessen the hold it has on me. I can just let it go once I have identified the feeling. I have been practicing this for almost thirty-five years, and it works for me. I know it will work for you, too.

10

My mom was diagnosed with dementia in 2008, but she kept it a secret.

In January of 2012, I got a phone call from the local nursing home telling me that my mother was up there saying all kinds of crazy things, and I told them it was very normal for her. The response was, "I work with geriatric patients every day, and this lady is very confused and doesn't know where she is. We called her sister and the police to escort her home." This was the beginning of nine long years with my mother.

In April of that year, we found ourselves in the emergency room. There had been a disturbance at the retirement home, and she had been sent to the ER. After many hours of questions and listening to stories I had never heard her tell, she agreed to go to a nearby behavioral unit. By 10:00 the next morning, she was trying to get a taxi to come get her and take her home, but the doctor at the behavioral unit had seen enough to know my mother needed help, so he had her committed.

After she was there for a few days, the doctor said she

could not go home and that she needed to be in assisted living so someone could take care of her. We found a place for her, and she fought us tooth and nail. One of my sisters heard about the AMEN clinic in Plano, Texas. They did something called a SPECT, which is a scan that can see what is going on in a person's brain. She was diagnosed with bi-polar disorder, chronic traumatic encephalopathy (CTE), dementia due to head trauma, mood disorder NOS, and PTSD.

She had lived her entire life with bi-polar disorder with no medication — no wonder she was the mother she was. She could not help her mood swings. She was either like Superman and able to leap tall buildings or she would lay in bed and sleep for days. I had studied my mother throughout my entire life, trying to figure out what was wrong with her. I went from thinking she was schizophrenic to bi-polar to having no idea what was wrong with her. I just knew something was wrong, and there was nothing I could do about it.

She escaped the assisted living facility, and we lived in sheer terror and anguish for the next nine years, not knowing what was going to happen next. It was a roller coaster ride that I never chose to get on.

I was afraid she would get in her truck and hit someone or kill a young man that had young children, leaving them fatherless and without someone to provide for them. She did not care. She wanted to drive, and she was going to get in her truck every day and drive where she wanted to drive. I prayed every day, "God please protect anyone that is on the road from my mother." You see, we legally could not take her vehicles away from her in our little town. But who would they blame if she actually did kill someone in her truck? That would be us. It was a battle we never won, so I lived in fear for a life that she might take.

For the next nine years, there was story after story that caused me so much pain. She would show up at my house for holidays just to make trouble. She had nothing good to say about anybody. She would tell my kids how I had taken everything from her — all of her money and land. You name it, and I had stolen it. This period of time was even harder than my growing up years. She was impossible.

I cried out to God again, "How is this going to end? God, please help me know what to do. I cannot take much more of this." I ran across a book entitled "Mothers Who Can't Love: A Healing Guide for Daughters" by Susan Forward. In the first half of the book, the author does an incredible job describing all the possible mothers a person could have, and in the last half of the book, she lays out what a person can do about it. It is your choice.

One of the choices was to walk away, and I had already decided that that was what I was going to have to do with my mother. I never had a decent conversation with her, even before the dementia set in, but it was ten times worse after. I hated to see her coming. If she was in the grocery store, I ran the other way. I just couldn't stand to see her. The author of this book gave me permission to do that, and I decided I had to think about my own sanity and my own health. I had to do what was good for me. I could not take care of my mother at this time, so I walked away.

By 2019, she had progressed to the point that something had to happen. Her truck was no longer usable, so she had no way to drive. She started walking everywhere she went. She was no longer taking care of herself when it came to things like bathing and personal hygiene. She would start walking, and someone would stop to pick her up, even after we had told her that if she needed something, we would come and get her. She was going to be in control, and she was going to do what she wanted to do.

Everyone in town was afraid of my mother because she was a very mean and hateful person, and they just let her do what she wanted to do. She was crazy, and everyone knew it. After this had gone on for a few months, I decided I could not stand by anymore. I got in contact with a behavioral unit that I heard would take care of my mother and knew how to handle people with dementia. The lady in the behavioral unit instructed me on what to do, and they would be ready for her. So my older sister and I tricked my mother to get her in the car — it was the only way — and took her to the behavioral unit. It was so hard, but they did take care of her.

It wasn't as simple as I am writing, and after many adventures and craziness, we finally got guardianship of her and placed her in the only home that would take her because she had become violent.

She went into that home in March of 2020, just as the lockdowns for the pandemic happened. We had no intention of putting her in a home and walking away. We were going to visit her three or four times a week. I had just retired, so I was going to have the time to do that. Unfortunately, we were not allowed to visit, and she went down fast. When we placed her, she was still singing and dancing, but by August, she could no longer. It was very sad to see. My mean, hateful mother was now confined to a wheelchair and barely knew who I was.

In January 2021, the home called because my mother had tested positive for COVID, and she would be placed on the wing where all the COVID patients were. She had a low-grade fever, and that was about it. She was so strong. After ten days, they put her back on her wing. I called and asked since she has had COVID, can we come see her? Two of my sisters had had COVID, so I didn't see what the big deal was. They had had it, and they had antibodies, but the answer was no.

We got together and decided when my sister went to see her the first week in February that she should bring her home. February 5th, 2021, my mother came home. I was shocked at the way she looked. We were paying that place $4000 a month to take care of my mom, and she looked like an old hag. She was a woman that got her hair done every week, and now her hair was long and stringy. The first thing I did before we put her to bed was cut her hair. Her finger-nails were a mile long and filthy. I was disgusted. I know God has a reason for everything, but that place did not take care of my mother.

We got her into bed, and I pulled a chair up and told her how beautiful she was. She looked me in the eye and thanked me. I knew she loved to sing, so I started singing "Amazing Grace," and she began to sing with me. She may not have recognized me, but she could remember all the words to that song.

I visited my mother, who I was now calling "Mom." Honestly, I called her "Mother" because she made me, but now, she was my mom. I would come and sit by the bed, and she would look at me and tell me how beautiful I was. Wow, my mother had never told me I was beautiful. Some days, I would come, and she would say, "When you kids were little, I was just so mad, I spanked you all day long, and you had not done anything wrong. I was just taking my anger out on you because I was mad at your daddy. I am so sorry I did that." She had never said she was sorry for anything.

For five months, I heard my mom tell me how beautiful I was and how sorry she was for what she had done. All that time, I had asked God how was this all going to end, and here was my answer.

My mother was a bitter, angry, hateful woman until the last five months of her life. By this time, she was also diagnosed with Alzheimer's disease as well as her other conditions. We were finally able to get her the help that was needed for her disorders, and because of that, she was the sweetest and kindest woman I had ever known. God was so gracious to give me five months with that version of her. She apologized to me all the time, and she had never apologized one day in her life because she was always right. She told me every day that I was beautiful. Every day that I went to see her, I told her she was beautiful and I loved her so much. I loved my mother!

My mother lived to be 91, and my love for her from when I was three returned when I was sixty-eight. There is nothing I would trade for those five months with my mom. My God is a God of redemption, and He redeemed my relationship with her the way only He could. It would have been okay if He hadn't, but I am so grateful that now when I think of my mom, I can smile at the memories we shared in the end. Forgiveness was, and is, a beautiful gift to me.

AFTERWORD

To survive my upbringing, I had to become invisible, and I still feel that way sometimes today. Though I've been in leadership positions for decades, I never saw myself as a leader. The beatings my confidence experienced prevented me from being able to truly see myself as God saw me.

But this story is not about how awful my mother was. It's a story of how human she was. She had her demons, and she had her difficulties, and she really struggled as a person. And I think I inherited my ability to hear from God from my mother. Both can be true, and one does not invalidate the other. Loving an abuser is complicated. There's no right or wrong way to do it.

In the same way, my daddy was absent for most of my childhood, and I also fell in love with him when I left for school. I got to know him on a completely different level and was able to build a wonderful relationship with him.

I suppose, in the end, a person is not just their worst day or their best day.

I have the gift of being able to look at the memories of my mother and very clearly see the broken woman she was.

Yes, she made my life a living hell. Yes, she caused me more hardship than anyone on the planet ever did. And yet, I can see the broken little girl that she was, and I can separate that from the woman who terrorized me as a child.

I get to choose how I experience the memories of my mother. She wasn't a saint, and she wasn't the devil. She wasn't a demon, and she wasn't an angel. She was a flawed human being, and though most of my childhood was really difficult, there were some very special days with my mother that I am able to still cherish.

Southerners love to quote the Bible and say that we should honor thy father and thy mother so that your life will be long in the land (Exodus 20:12), and I used to think to myself, "Wait a minute. I have nothing to honor my mother for. She lies, she's mean, she's hateful. What do I have to respect about her?"

God sat me down and said, "Yes, Judy, you're right. Your mother's awful. But she gave you life. If it hadn't been for her, you would not exist. You are who you are because of your parents."

So that's where I started. There was nothing else I could honor her for, so I focused on the fact that she gave me life. That was the beginning of me seeing her beyond the horrible things she had done and the terrible person that she was.

Once I understood that her behavior wasn't my fault, I was able to release a little more and continue seeing her as a human being and not just a big, bad awful person who treated me so poorly.

I was reading a story about a man who had been abandoned by his father, and he was going to find his dad and tell him how angry he was with him. He found his grave instead, and he stood there and screamed at his father for leaving him as a baby. Gradually, he changed his mind and decided to send him love instead. As I was telling someone this impactful story, she turned to me and said, "Judy, don't you think that could be your story, too, about your mom?" That was the moment, at fifty years old, that I started sending my mother love. Even when she said ugly things to me, I'd send her love.

There were years I had to walk away and not have conversations with her at all. Like I said, loving an abuser is complicated. I'd still pray for her and send her love anyway — just from a safe distance.

Your story with your parents is not over yet. It didn't end at 18 when you became an adult. It could be really messy right now and feel irreparable, but there is always hope if you want it. Maybe you don't ever want to repair the relationship, and that's okay, too. But if any part of you does desire reconciliation, may my story bring you the hope you need that it's possible to have a broken and abusive relationship with your parents for your entire life and still get your own five-month experience and be able to draw on those new memories after their passing.

God is a God of healing and restoration, and if He can restore my relationship with my mother, He can restore yours, too. I had prayed for a new family throughout my entire childhood, and it's only been in the last six months that I realized He did answer that prayer. He gave me my college family and then my own family. I have a beautiful relationship with each of my children, and I know that would never have been possible without healing. What a beautiful revelation that's been for me.

A close friend once told me that I see God so much in my life, and my focus is on Him and pleasing Him so much that she and others just sneak in behind me and do the same thing. I'd like to think that the same can be said about the way I've healed from my childhood. I hope that after reading this book, you know that your healing is possible, too. I hope you realize that no matter what you choose to do regarding your abusive parent(s), the best thing you can ever do for yourself is to heal and choose joy.

If I can leave you with any final thoughts, it would be this:

What happened to me as a child wasn't my fault, but healing from it was, and continues to be, my responsibility. The same is true of you.

ACKNOWLEDGMENTS

I would first like to thank my daughter, Alicia van Rijn, who invited me to participate in a project that she was participating in. It was writing a book chapter for Lauren da Silva. The topic was something I could speak to so I reached out to Lauren and was accepted to write that book chapter. I want to thank Lauren for accepting me to be a part of that project. After writing my chapter, I felt disconnected from the group and to the whole process, so I reached out to Alicia again and she told me that Lauren had a vault in Facebook that would explain everything. So, I went to the vault and listened to everything Lauren had posted and that is where I met Meggan Larson. I contacted Meggan immediately because I felt God's call on my life to write this book. Thank you so much Meggan, Lauren, and Alicia for making this dream come true without you it would still be a dream.

ABOUT THE AUTHOR

Judy Taylor is a wife, mother, grandmother, loyal friend, Bible study leader, and author who lives in Daingerfield, Texas. She is a mastermind leader, speaker, and coach with John Maxwell and a retired mathematics professor from a small Christian university. Her desire is to see women everywhere heal from the traumas in their lives while she comes alongside them to give them a hand up.

You can reach Judy through her website at johnmaxwellgroup.com/judytaylor or e-mail at: judyt10241953@gmail.com

ALSO BY JUDY TAYLOR

Being & Belonging Anthology